SOFT-STYLE CONSCIOUS AWAKENING

A BEING THIS-HERE-NOW PLAYBOOK

GARY CROWLEY

Arasmas Publications

CONTENTS

PREFACE

Dear Reader,

As best you can, dive into the material that follows. A graceful swan dive is lovely, but an enthusiastic belly flop will do just as well. Immersing yourself is the best way to get where you're going. Plus, it's more fun.

Toe-dippers seldom get the essence of these teachings because they stay on the surface, and that's precisely how the false self, the *Imaginary You*, remains unaffected.

So, whenever you're ready, let's dive in!

Shall we?

1

TRUE PLACES

"IT'S NOT DOWN IN ANY MAP; TRUE PLACES NEVER ARE," wrote Herman Melville in his book *Moby Dick*.

He was referring to the character Queequeg's native island of Rokovoko. Its exact location, described as, "an island far away to the West and South," leaves even an expert explorer plenty of room to fail at finding the actual island.

If you yearned to visit the seldom experienced Isle of Rokovoko, you could find a maritime historian who could give you lots of second-hand information on how to navigate there. Even better, you could chat with a crusty old seafarer who had been there and could report his real-life experiences to you.

But better still would be to find a captain who had sailed his boat there, and had also successfully guided others on the journey to Rokovoko. This last option would make your chances of finding Rokovoko the very best of all.

The spiritual seeker could apply these same criteria to their journey. There are those that can talk about conscious awakening from what they've read and heard, and that can be helpful. And there are those that are there, or at least have *been* there, that can tell you even more about it from a place of actual experiencing.

Then there are those who are there now, and that have also guided others to a conscious awakening. It's these teachers and their teachings that are most likely to successfully guide you there as well.

Like Rokovoko, the path to a conscious awakening may not be drawn on any map, but some do know how to show you the way there.

As the story usually goes with *true places*, the Captain will inevitably head in a direction different than you expected to be going. And this is why true places are so difficult to find. He'll begin the journey heading due north, even though everyone knows Rokovoko is, "West and to the South."

When you inquire as to why he's headed north, he'll reply, "Going north runs us directly into the path of the migrating grey whales. They swim past the shores of Rokovoko twice a year. It's the only sure way to find the tiny isle."

Suddenly, a seemingly mysterious and complicated journey has turned into a simple *noticing*. Just notice the whales and follow their lead.

Our journey to your conscious awakening is similar. We may head in a direction opposite from what you supposed. And much like the surest way to Roko-voko, we're just on a journey of noticing. We'll notice what *is* and what *is not* and go where that takes us.

Rest assured, the direction we go has worked for many before us on these spiritual seas, so do your best to enjoy the ride. This is, after all, a *play*book, so I hope you've come ready to play!

THE RIGHT QUESTIONS ARE THE ANSWER

Experiencing, Experiencing, Experiencing

IF WE GRANTED SUPERHERO STATUS TO TEACHERS, THEN language teacher Michel Thomas would have taught his lessons wearing a red cape and blue leotards.

The results he achieved with his students is the stuff of legend.

Was his success due to his students being held to a higher standard for achievement than others? Well, it couldn't have been that because the first thing Michel Thomas would tell his students is that if they made a mistake, it was the teacher's fault; *not* the student's.

Was Michel Thomas so successful because his students were all intensely focused and taking copious notes? No, that couldn't be it either, since his students were seated in big comfortable lounge chairs in a dimly lit room, and weren't even allowed to take notes.

Was it because he only worked with the best and the brightest language students? That couldn't have been it. He often worked with people who had convinced themselves that they couldn't learn a second language, or those that other teachers had given up on entirely.

Teachers consider Michel Thomas a superhero among teachers because he could teach someone, almost anyone, five years' worth of French (or, incidentally, seven other languages) in 3 days.

The students' only job was to stay relaxed during class. No stress allowed was the golden rule.

He would then teach them French in the tiniest, most easily digestible simple words or phrases in French that you can imagine. Then he would ask the students, "So, how do you say _____?" which the students would then repeat back.

Each small morsel was something anyone could learn, so there was no reason to worry about it too much.

Each tiny piece of new language could be easily repeated back to the teacher whenever he asked them how to say the words or phrase; as could the tiny piece they had learned a moment earlier; as could the tiny piece they would learn a minute after that.

Each thin slice lay effortlessly upon the next, so that at the end of the three days the students could speak median level conversational French.

The power of Michel Thomas's teaching method was in the fact that the students were *experiencing* French for three consecutive days. They were not just thinking about French language concepts. They were speaking French in very small chunks that happened to coalesce flawlessly into a conversational structure.

Michel Thomas provided an *experiential assist* in the speaking of French.

The students were immersed in an unusually relaxed experiencing of a foreign language, because each micro introduction of new information didn't need to be overthought. And even if they did forget a word or phrase, it was simple enough to repeat back to them what they had forgotten, and everything would fall nicely back into place.

The students never got too far off track because they were *experiencing* the new language. They were never too far from a lesson being easily re-experienced, and they were completely absorbed in the experiencing of speaking French.

This constant *experiencing* is what I wish for the spiritual seeker, who so very often ends up on the hamster wheel of concepts, and misses out on the joy of experiencing what the concepts are pointing toward.

My hope is that you will *play* with the material in this *play*book, and have an actual conscious awakening—an experiencing of *this-here-now*—*as* what you *are*.

It's also my hope that you understand the mechanisms that allowed your conscious awakening to occur, so you can revisit that experiencing again, and again, and again . . . until it's where you naturally abide ... *as* the *conscious experiencing* of *Oneness* that *you are*.

Let the games begin!

Questions and Answers - Knowing the Difference Makes All the Difference

Seeking a conscious awakening is a lot like learning French, learning to ride a bicycle, or learning to swim, in at least one regard; experiential learning is the best way to go.

The time has come for you to get wet. Swan dive or belly flop, it's up to you, but we're going in.

I'm going to ask you a few simple questions. Just take a few seconds and answer them as best you can. Here we go:

Easy Questions

- Do you have a headache right now?

- Have you ever flown on an airplane?

- What noises can you hear right now?

- What do you see in front of you right now?

- Have you ever been to the North Pole?

- Have you ever been to the Grand Canyon?

- Is your left foot experiencing pain at this moment?

- Do you have pink nail polish on any of your fingernails? Toenails?

Okay . . . that wasn't so hard, right?

No matter how you answered these questions, you based them on your actual experiencing of things, so the answers were easy.

Now, let me ask you a few more questions:

- Can you recall a pleasant memory from your childhood? Take a moment to notice what you like about that memory.

- Can you think of another pleasant memory from another time in your life? Take a moment and notice what you like about that memory as well.

With all the questions I've asked so far, all you've had to do was focus your attention in the direction of your experiencing. It didn't matter if the experiencing was from the past, or from the present; you just noticed what you noticed, and reported back the answer.

All you had to do was dive into your experiencing, and the answers were right there in your experiencing, ripe for the picking. Easy peasy lemon squeezy! Yes?

"Look Mom, no concepts required! Just my experiencing."

Difficult Questions

Now I want you to answer some more questions. Take a few seconds with each one—not *too* long—but do respond in *some* way, even if you think it's not a very good answer.

- What is non-duality?

- What is a conscious awakening?

- How long does it take to awaken?

- What happens when we die?

- What does, "You are already enlightened," mean?

- Ask yourself, "Who am I?" What's your answer?

- What does, "I Am That," mean?

What was it like for you to answer those questions? Were they more difficult for you to answer than the previous ones?

Did you find yourself *experiencing* the answers like you did with the first set of questions I asked you? Or were your answers more conceptual; more thinking-based than experiencing-based?

Did you notice that the more difficult questions led to answers that tended to branch out into even more concepts?

If I gave you more time with each question, can you see how those concepts could easily lead to more concepts . . . and then more concepts . . . with a great possibility that you will *never* get to the actual *experiencing* of what these concepts are all pointing toward?

Can you see how these *hard-style* questions are like a mythical Hydra, where every time you cut off one head, seven more heads grow back?

This is how seekers end up with *Multiple Spiritual Concepts Disorder* (MSCD). This syndrome is not officially recognized by the medical community, or the non-dual community, but I've seen it.

MSCD is when the seeker ends up with so *many* concepts rolling around in their head that they get stuck in the dualist world of concepts. They're not sure if they're everything or nothing, the absolute or the relative, awareness or consciousness, an *I*, a *Me*, or an *I Am*; in a dream, or in reality, etc., etc.

And talking about all these spiritual concepts just creates more Hydras; more immediate concepts, and more potential spiritual concepts.

So what's a seeker to do?

Water Anyone?

There's an old saying of mystics and sages that all they're ever doing is, "selling water by the river's edge." In other words, they're teaching you what is always freely available to you right where you already are.

But notice that the mystics and sages didn't say they were selling water by the *ocean's* edge. That's because not all water is the same when it comes to quenching your thirst.

If you're ever adrift at sea in a lifeboat, the very first

rule for survival is, "No matter how thirsty you get, don't drink the saltwater."

That's because it takes your kidneys more water to eliminate all of the salt in saltwater than the amount of water in the seawater itself. So the more saltwater you drink, the more dehydrated and thirsty you become.

Water for the human body is much like spiritual concepts for the spiritual seeker. Spiritual concepts can seem to quench a deep thirst within you. But in the long run, are they quenching your thirst, or making you thirstier? Recognizing the difference is critical.

Let's take a closer look.

Soft-Style vs. Hard-Style

Take a moment and notice the difference in your experiencing when you answer these two questions:

> In this moment, does your foot hurt?
> versus
> What is *the absolute* in non-duality?

When I ask about your foot, your attention is steered toward focusing on your foot. You have a present moment experiencing of your foot. And then you notice if your foot is hurting. Only then do you report back with whatever you noticed.

When I ask you about, "the absolute," where does

your attention go? The question gets tossed into the *concept manufacturing factory* known as *the mind*, and it goes to work creating concepts for you in an attempt to figure out an answer.

Many of those concepts that the mind generates may be very well thought out. They may be stunning in their brilliance and light up the intellectual debates on the non-duality internet forums.

But if those brilliant concepts don't lead to a present moment experiencing of that toward which they point, then they won't help you awaken.

It's like drinking saltwater; the concepts seem like they're quenching your spiritual thirst, but they're really just making you thirstier. The seeker has to be careful or they'll just end up chugging a lot a saltwater over a lifetime of seeking.

The questions that steer you into conceptualizing are what I term *hard-style* questions because you're doing things the hard way.

They may be interesting questions. They may be fun to chat about or debate, and there's nothing wrong with that. But if there's no experiencing accompanying the concepts, then it's just entertainment. And entertainment is fine, as long as you know that's all you're getting.

Let's do this soft-style versus hard-style comparison

again. Try these two questions and compare what happens:

Are you cold at the moment?
versus
What is a *conscious awakening*?

The first question brings you into the present moment experiencing where you merely report back what you notice. The second question ignites the manufacturing of more concepts, which are dualistic by nature, and make it harder to see through the illusion of separateness.

And yes, concepts are also part of your present moment experiencing and are not separate from you, but they're not the actual experiencing they point toward.

You can try and quench your thirst with the word *water* written down on a piece of paper, but it falls quite short when compared to the experiencing of drinking a tall, cool glass of mountain spring water.

Soft-Style Funneling

The key to conscious awakening is to experientialize your concepts about Awakening.

Concepts are dualist by nature. They're labels that define something as *this* versus something else defined as *that*. And since concepts are the only tools we have to communicate with, we should clarify how we can best utilize them.

Funneling is the term I use to describe the taking of a concept and spinning it down into an actual experiencing for the seeker.

So, let's take the classic non-dual question, "Who Am I?" Seekers have spent decades asking themselves this question without cracking the code.

Here's an exchange where this question gets funneled down into experiencing:

Seeker: So, who am I? I mean, ultimately, *Who Am I?*

Gary: Who wants to know?

Seeker: Me, I guess.

Gary: And who seems to be the *me* in that location? (It may only be a *seems to be*, but this very *seems to be* is the actual *experiencing* they can honestly report).

Seeker: *Sam*

Gary: So it seems like there's a *Sam* in that location. And this *Sam* would like an answer to this question, "Who am I?" Is that correct?

Seeker: Yes.

Gary: Can we look for a *Sam* to see if we can actually find a *Sam*?

Seeker: I know there's no *Sam*.

Gary: Oh, so you've been around non-duality a little while. Okay—well, I know that *intellectually* you know there's no *Sam*. But can we actually look for a *Sam* and see if we can find this *seems to be* a *Sam*? Just to make sure there isn't a *Sam* somewhere?

Seeker: But I've looked before and never found one, so I already know there isn't one.

Gary: Hmm, I think your *knowing* is more of a believed thought. But I tend to be really in favor of actual experiencing, so would you indulge me and just look again to see if you can find a *Sam*? Who knows? We might actually find one.

Seeker: Okay.

Gary: Great. Let's start by searching through the body. I want you to scan your feet and tell me if this *seems to be* you we call *Sam* is in your feet. Is there a *Sam* in there?

Seeker: No. I can't find a *Sam* in my feet.

Gary: Scan your shins and tell me, is this *seems to be* a *Sam* in your shins?

Seeker: No.

This questioning continues as we investigate (experientially investigate!) and actually actively look for the one who seems to want the answer to the question,

"Who Am I?" The question is answered experientially by the seeker when they experientially can't find the one that *seems* to want an answer.

With a soft-style approach, the seeker's questions are not solved. Their questions are *dissolved*.

Many of us have heard the classic teacher's response to common non-duality questions: *Who wants to know?*

It's a great response to shut down the manufacturing of more concepts that are not going to help the seeker. But an opportunity for the seeker has been missed if the questioning by the teacher doesn't then funnel down into a conscious, present moment experiencing of what's being taught.

Here's another example:

Seeker: I've been at this for years, and all I want to know is how do I get to experience non-separate consciousness?

Gary: Who is it that doesn't want to be separate?

Seeker: Me, this person named Sharon.

Gary: So there's a separate entity we call Sharon who wants to have an experiencing of non-separateness?

Seeker: I guess so.

Gary: No guessing.

Seeker: Yes, Sharon wants an experiencing of non-separateness.

Gary: I'm a bit suspicious about this *seems to be* separate Sharon. Do you mind if we look around a bit to see if we can find an *actual* Sharon?

Seeker: Okay, let's look for a Sharon.

Gary: Great, let's experientially investigate and see if we can find a Sharon. Can you notice a place in the body where a *Sharon* seems to be? Take your time and look around.

The seeker, *Sharon*, had a perfectly reasonable question. It's a very common one in the world of non-duality. And any question is always an opportunity to funnel the seeker down into a present moment experiencing of that which they are seeking.

If you only sit around exchanging concepts, you're merely moving dualistic chess pieces around the chessboard of a *seems to be* separate, dualistic experiencing.

The seeker has a dualistic lens on experiencing. This is why they're still a spiritual seeker. When they use dualistic concepts to try and shift that experiencing into a non-dual experiencing, it's only natural that questions will arise.

This set-up is like trying to dry off with a wet towel

while you're still standing in the pouring rain. Tricky doesn't even begin to describe it.

If the teachings you study can't get you to hop on the ride of actually experiencing non-dual consciousness, then all their gorgeous concepts are just chatter. It's like listening to a waiter describe a restaurant's delicious food, but never bringing it to the table so you can taste it.

> *The conscious experiencing of non-separateness is just that—an experiencing!*

So you won't consciously have the experiencing of non-separateness unless you're steered away from identifying with all those very enticing spiritual concepts.

∼

Summary

This short chapter laid a critical foundation for the spiritual seeker. Soft-style teaching steers the seeker to report on the experiencing of *what is*. Hard-style teaching steers the seeker to conceptualize the experiencing they're aiming toward.

When attempting to navigate to a *true place* that has been difficult for others to find, you may have to go in a different direction than the one most people would assume to be the right way.

The legendary French teacher, Michel Thomas, gave us a clue that effortlessly digestible, bite-sized pieces of experiencing, each one neatly stacked upon the next, can be a very powerful way of teaching. This experiential *soft-style* can have miraculous effects; effects other *styles* might consider to be impossible.

With hard-style seeking, the seeker asks questions and the teacher gives answers. Generally, this version of seeking manufactures endless concepts that the seeker can then spend a lifetime wading through, without ever actually awakening.

By definition, the seeker's experiencing is dualistic, thus the seeker can't help but ask dualist based questions.

Even though the teacher is giving answers based on their non-dual experiencing, those answers will be interpreted through the seeker's dualistic lens on experiencing. It just doesn't work very well, which is why I call it *hard-style*.

Answers have the appearance of being very powerful, especially those so eloquently given by truly wonderful teachers. And there's nothing that appears so weak, so unimpressive, as a simple question. Yet the *right* questions are capable of overcoming the strongest of your illusions, which is why the *soft-style* approach is so effective.

The *right* questions are truly the answer the seeker has been looking for. It's only the right questions that can funnel the seeker down into experiencing. And it's only in *experiencing*—not *conceptualizing*—that awakening can occur.

This understanding is so profound for the seeker that it can't be emphasized enough. This is how you pick the lock on the *gateless gate*; you *experience* your way through it because the *gate* is made of *concepts*. First and foremost, the concept of an *Imaginary You* is the gateless gate!

Let's begin the soft-style process of seeing through the Imaginary You, shall we?

THE EXPERIENTIAL JOY OF PMI

The Unassuming Question

COLUMBO WAS A DETECTIVE SHOW ON TELEVISION WHEN I
was a child. Each week, Lieutenant Columbo would
drive up to a crime scene in a beat-up old convertible,
accompanied by his basset hound named *Dog*. By all
appearances, he was a disheveled, dull-minded
little man.

Scratching his head with a cigar in hand, he seemed
easily distracted, even befuddled as he examined each
crime scene. Always underselling himself, he'd say
things to suspects like, "My wife says I'm the second
smartest guy she knows. She claims there are 80 guys
tied for first."

Each week he attempted to solve crimes committed by
brilliant criminals. His entire way of being completely
disarmed his suspects who undoubtedly felt their

meticulously planned crimes were no match for such a doddering old fool. But Columbo's soft genius was in the seemingly innocent questions he would ask.

"Oh, Sir, just *one* more thing . . ." was his classic opener.

"That's quite a typewriter. Would you mind showing me how it works?" or, "As a wine expert, could I ask you the best way to store a nice bottle of wine?" were questions his suspects deigned to answer.

His simple questions were like water seeping into the cracks of a concrete foundation. Without making a ripple, such softness can undermine the entire structure of a building.

The unassuming questions Columbo asked would find their way into the cracks in the criminal's story. Questions that appeared to be a mere afterthought, something barely worth mentioning, would end up undoing the most brilliant seeming villains.

Columbo knew how to ask the *right* questions, just like we're going to ask the right questions in the *Present Moment Investigations* that follow. The questions may not seem like much at first; they may even seem like no more than a curiosity; but make no mistake, they're the *right* questions despite their simplistic appearance.

All the while, the integrity of the false self is gently undermined. The persistent but fragile illusion of the

Imaginary You is dissolved, without anyone really noticing until it's gone.

Is Present Moment Investigation (or PMI) the *Columbo* of spiritual teachings?

I guess it's time we found out.

Present Moment Investigation (PMI)

A Note to the Reader:
It's generally most effective to read the rest
of this chapter in one sitting if possible.

WHEN I WAS 18 years old, my Tae Kwan Do instructor, Master Kim, would say at least three times every hour, "The basics are very, very important," in his heavily accented English. It turns out that he was right in any language—the basics *are* very, very important—for almost all the things we wish to master in this life.

Awakening, too, is all about the basics.

Non-dual conscious awakening is an experiencing. It's not a conceptualizing. That's why PMI is intended to funnel you down into the experiencing of the present moment as what you *are*, which is the essence of conscious awakening.

Before we begin, I'd like to note a few things.

First, PMI is intended to investigate the present moment. The present moment may include memories of the past or imaginings of the future, but even these are present moment experiencings. No matter what illusions or delusions the present moment may contain, it's still *present moment* experiencing.

Second, PMI is an investigation. It's not just an intellectual *inquiry*. PMI is intended to drive home the paramount importance of *actual experiential investigation* of the questions presented. Even when you think you know the answer to what we're investigating, even if you've, "Done this all before," it's important to do the experiential investigation.

It's the experiencing of the investigation that brings you not to the place where the questions of the false self are *solved*, but to the place where the questions of the false self are *dissolved*.

If I could only pick one thing for you to take away from this playbook it would be that the spiritual seeker understands the game-changing importance of experientially investigating the present moment. Just *intellectually* inquiring about the present moment won't get the job done.

And then after your first awakening, you must continue to experientially investigate the present moment, until you naturally abide as the moment itself.

Try not to overthink what we're doing in the pages that follow. Do your best to stick to the investigations as I present them below. You'll have all the time in the world to think about them after we're done.

Lastly, remember that there's quite literally nothing you can do wrong as a spiritual seeker (or otherwise; but we'll get to that later), so do your best to just relax and enjoy the journey.

The PMI Sequence

Take a moment and look at your surroundings. What do you see? What objects can you point out? Is there a chair, a picture, a lamp that you are experiencing? If you're outside, is there a tree, a house, or a street that you are experiencing?

Take a brief moment and notice what separate objects you see in this present moment.

Now, if I were to ask you who you experientially *seem to be* in this present moment, what would your answer be? I'm not looking for some spiritual answer; I want to know what it's *really* like for you *experientially* as you look out at those objects in your environment.

Do you experientially feel like a separate self?

Do you feel like a separate being with a particular name that others would identify as *You*?

Do you experientially feel like a separate self that lives in a particular place and has unique tastes, talents, and opinions?

Does it seem like you're an independent self who's making conscious decisions that have brought you to this particular place and time?

Is your experiencing that other human beings seem like other separate selves? Does it seem like they're also making conscious decisions that bring them to the places they happen to be at any given moment in time?

If your experiencing seems anything like the separate self-described above then welcome to a not so small club called *the vast majority of humanity*. That's about seven billion people, and it's the only kind of experiencing that most of them will ever have.

But if you're reading this book, you've probably already become suspicious about this *seemingly separate self*. And here you are!

So let's look into this seemingly separate self and see if we can find out not just, "What's going on?" but first and foremost, "What's *not* going on?"

The questions that follow are being asked to you, the reader, so I hope you'll play along and answer them. I chose to use the unisex name *Sam* as a filler so just plug your name in below wherever you see the word *Sam*.

Do your best to *do* this process with me—don't just *read* about it—the benefits will definitely be worth the effort.

Step 1: Just Noticing What's Going On

Let's begin with some simple noticing.

In a moment, I'm going to ask you to notice a few things with your eyes closed, but first read the short description of what you're going to be asked to notice. Once you understand what you're being asked to notice, just close your eyes and begin noticing.

With your eyes closed, take a full minute and notice whatever experiencing is occurring, without trying to control any of it. Notice whatever thoughts come and go. Notice whatever sounds you experience and whatever body sensations you notice. Just noticing the experiencing, whatever that experiencing may be, for a full minute is all we're going to do.

Now, go ahead and take a minute to do the *noticing* described above. I'll wait.

All done? Good.

Did you notice that there's lots of experiencing going

on? Lots of thoughts, sounds, and physical feelings going on all the time . . .

And did you notice that you didn't have to do anything at all for that experiencing to go on?

The experiencing of living is just happening, without a *You* having to do anything at all. Right?

Great, so we can agree that the experiencing of living can go on without anyone having to *do* anything to make it happen, or anyone needing to control it. Yes?

Now, take a full minute with your eyes open and look around. Notice all the experiencing, without judging or trying to control it. Just relax into the noticing of all the experiencing that's going on.

Go ahead and do it. I'll wait.

Did you do it? Good.

Did you notice that with your eyes open there's even more experiencing going on than with your eyes closed? Did you notice it's just happening all on its own without a separate *You* needing to do anything?

Great—so the experiencing of living is something that goes on without any separate *You* needing to *do* something to make it happen. That's a pretty good noticing.

I guess the next question is that if the experiencing of living is already going on anyway, what does a *Sam* add to the experiencing?

Step 2: The Park Bench Test

Imagine for a moment that you're sitting on a park bench on a beautiful spring day. As you enjoy the warmth of the spring sun and the sounds of nature all around you, you notice your longtime friend walking down the pathway toward you.

Now, let me ask you this; when the friend looks over at your physical body, they'll see a *Sam*, right?

Great, so your friend would look at your body and see a *Sam*. No news there.

But now imagine the same scene, you sitting on the park bench, but this time it's a complete stranger walking your way.

When that stranger looks over at you, will they see a *Sam*?

No, the stranger won't be able to see a *Sam*, will they?

So, what *will* the stranger see when they glance at you?

They will only be able to see a nameless body. Right?

And why can't they see a *Sam*?

They can't see a *Sam* because no one has told them your *story*; the thoughts in their head that would allow them to imagine a separate and independent character called *Sam*. Right again?

Your friend has all sorts of thoughts and stories based on behavioral patterns and events that he ties to the body he thinks of as *Sam*. Still right?

Both the friend and the stranger can see your body; no doubt about that, correct?

But only your friend can see a *Sam*. True?

Now imagine that I took you to a busy sidewalk in a city where you didn't know anyone.

Would everyone who walks past be able to see your body?

Yes, everyone would be able to see your body. Right?

Would any stranger who walks by you on that sidewalk be able to see a *Sam*?

No, no stranger would be able to see a Sam. Right again?

So would it be fair to say that these human bodies are objective things in our relative world that everyone can see? Yes?

Yes, bodies are objective things that everyone can see. On that we can all agree.

Would it also be fair to say that the thoughts that would allow someone to imagine an independent character tied to a body called *Sam* would be more of a subjective thing?

Yes, they're subjective. They are thoughts in some-one's head. Still yes?

So then, would it be fair to say that your physical body seems like an objective thing, but the idea of a *Sam* is more of a subjective thing?

Would it also be fair to say that *Sam* is more of a story? Actually, more like just thoughts about a *Sam* in some-one's head?

Yes?

Yes, that's why different people have different thoughts in their heads that they tie to different bodies.

Sam seems more like a subjective thing, like a collec-tion of ideas about *Sam* in people's head. Right?

Would it be more accurate to say that our physical body is one thing, and a *Sam* is another thing? *And* that they are *not* the same thing?

Yes, it would. Wouldn't it?

So the physical body and a Sam are *not* the same thing. Agreed?

Great. So let's take a closer look at these bodies and this idea of a *Sam*.

Let's investigate and make sure that the *Sam* that's, "Just an idea, just a story," in your friend's head, isn't it also, "Just an idea, just a story," in *your* head too?

Because WOW! That would change everything. If it's true . . .

Step 3: Sam's Performance Review

We know everyone can see your body, right?

Perfect strangers and longtime friends can see your body. True?

Terrific. So the fact that the body exists in our world is not in question here at all. Correct?

I also don't doubt for a second that it really *seems* like there's a *Sam* running the show. The *seeming* to be a *Sam* is never in question. We never, ever, ever question that a *Sam* seems to be in charge.

What's in question is the *actuality* of a *Sam* that's in control of the experiencing of living that goes on in the location of your body.

For instance, I don't mean to be rude, but I think it's time we check on *Sam's* competency for a moment. We'll just take notice of how good a job we think *Sam* is doing.

We'll do nothing more than notice some things in your own experiencing.

Let's do some thought watching for a moment. Just sit back for a full minute and notice the thoughts that are flowing through your experiencing. Take the *full* minute and just notice all of the thoughts wandering by.

Go ahead . . .

Okay . . . you probably noticed a pretty random bunch of thoughts after a full minute of thought watching, yes?

If your experiencing is like everyone else's, thoughts just appear with no rhyme or reason, and you have no idea what your next thought will be.

Now add this to your thought watching: Pick one very specific thought. Pick any thought you'd like.

Do you have one specific thought you've chosen?

Yes? Good.

Now, take the next full minute and ask *Sam* to think of only that thought, and that thought only. Notice if other thoughts creep in anyway. For instance, don't think of a pink elephant during this minute because that would be a thought other than the thought you picked. So pink elephants are definitely off limits and not to be thought about at all.

Okay. Here we go. Take another full minute and only think about your chosen thought. I'll do it with you.

So, how did you do? I lasted about a second before I noticed the birds chirping, and from then on it was a constant battle to get back to my chosen thought. Lots of other thoughts flowed in and out of my experiencing during that one minute.

And then, of course, the pink elephant kept popping in to show me that I truly don't control what thoughts come and go in my head.

Was it pretty similar for you? I suspect it was.

Okay, so a *Sam*, who's supposedly in charge of your experiencing of living, can't even control your thoughts. That's rather disappointing, I must say. I had much higher hopes for *Sam*. I thought he was in control of everything.

But remember, we're not here to pick on poor ole' *seems to be* a *Sam*. We're just here to notice what *is* and what *is not*.

Having fun yet?

Let's see what else we can notice.

Can you recall a time when you didn't want to be anxious, or angry, or depressed, or confused but you were anyway? And then you stayed stuck in that state for a lot longer than you would have liked to?

Most of us have no desire to feel anything considered *negative*, but it's something that happens to most of us at one time or another during our experiencing of living.

So riddle me this: If there seems to be a *Sam* in control

of our experiencing, it only makes sense that a *Sam* would not make a *Sam* feel the way a *Sam* doesn't want to feel, right?

I think it's a fair question. If there really was a *Sam* in charge of a *Sam*, how could you ever have sustained feelings that a *Sam* didn't want to have?

When we don't take the time to notice our actual experiencing of living in which thoughts and feelings just seem to come and go with no *Sam* in charge, we'll always be trying to get a *Sam* to fix things.

Seriously, if a *Sam* were in control *at all* we might have minor blips of negative feelings and emotions, but then *Sam* would rush in immediately and restore all the good feelings *Sam* wants. Right?

But we can notice from our own experiencing that this notion of a *Sam* in control of our emotions is just not the case.

So what's the point of having a *Sam* at all if *Sam* can't even make us feel good when we want to feel good? Seriously, I'm asking.

In your personal experiencing, can you recall a time, maybe after reading some great spiritual book, when a *Sam* desperately wanted to feel differently about *Sam* and the world?

Maybe a *Sam* wanted to be all loving, or compassion-ate, or in constant gratitude, or just fully accepting of everyone and everything they encounter? Did a *Sam* ever do that for you?

If you dip into the memory banks of your experiencing, can you notice a time when a *Sam* gave you all the feelings you wanted to feel all the time? Even for just a year or two?

No? Well, not for Imaginary Gary either, so don't feel too bad. It can be quite disappointing.

(Looking from here, I can certainly recall doing many, many hours of spiritual practices aimed at being all loving, fully compassionate, and absolutely accepting of each moment. And even with dedicated practice, a supposed *Gary*, that's seemingly in charge of how *I* feel, didn't make those things happen.)

It doesn't seem to be asking too much of a *Sam* that's in control of who and how you are to be able to make those loving, compassionate, and accepting feelings be your continual experiencing; I mean . . . that's what *Sam* wanted . . . *right*?

Yet you can easily notice that this hasn't happened in your own experiencing. And to be clear, we're not asking for world peace here—we're asking someone who's seemingly in control of *how* you are, to control *how you are*—why is that so hard?

In your experiencing, have you ever noticed good ole' *Sam* coming through on these simple desires? I think it's pretty clear the answer is a big *No*. Otherwise, you wouldn't be reading this book.

Here's a news flash: Everyone's version of *seems to be* a *Sam* fails miserably at fulfilling such simple desires. I'm not willing to call *Sam* an abject failure, but at best, *Sam* is a serious underachiever.

Sam may just be an idea that keeps us caught in the illusion of separateness. Wouldn't that be a kick in the pants to find out after all these years of seeking that *Sam* is just a thought in your head?

This *seems to be* a *Sam* is looking more and more suspect, so it's probably time we go and have an actual look for how this *seems to be* a *Sam* came to be part of our human experiencing.

Let's start at the very beginning, shall we?

Step 4: The Birth of Imaginary You

Let's take a moment and imagine the day your body was born. You've just popped out of your mother's womb; a little body that will grow into the adult body everyone will call *Sam*.

There's your little body, all fresh and screaming, laying on a table as they clean it up before they hand it over to your mother.

And now it's time for the doctor to fill out the birth certificate. So answer me this; does the doctor just look over at the baby and say, "Oh, that's obviously a *Sam*, so *Sam* is what I'll write on the birth certificate,"?

No; the doctor can't tell you're a *Sam* just by looking at that baby. He has no thoughts in his head about that little person, no story about a *Sam*.

The doctor just sees a new body. So, to fill out the *name* section on the birth certificate, the doctor has to ask someone what thoughts in their heads the parents have decided to assign to this baby body. Agreed?

And just to be clear, does the *baby* think it's a *Sam* yet?

Nope. Even the baby doesn't think it's a *Sam* on the day it's born, right?

If it were otherwise, the doctor could just walk over to the baby body that will grow into the adult body holding this book and ask, "Who are you?" and that baby would reply, "Hi Doc, I'm Sam. I'm a Capricorn. I like slow walks on the beach at sunset, candlelit dinners, and snuggling in front of the fireplace on cold winter nights."

But we all know babies don't do that for many reasons; the first being that *they* don't think they're a *Sam* yet. Right?

The body that starts as a baby takes a rather long time to start believing it's a *Sam*. Actually, it takes about two years for that baby to start thinking it's a *Sam*.

The creation of a *Sam* comes about through a pretty

standard conspiracy. The baby comes into the world as undifferentiated consciousness. It just has experiencings without thinking or feeling like a separate self.

There's the experiencing of hunger, and the experiencing of feeling full. There's pleasure, and sometimes pain. There's a warm, squishy feeling in the diaper from time to time, and then more feelings when the body is washed and bathed.

But all those feelings are just experiencings. There is no *Sam* that considers the experiencings to be those of a separate *Sam*.

So, let's be crystal clear where we are right now; there's this baby body that's already having experiencings of its own. The body comes first. And then there's this idea of a *Sam* that develops later. Yes?

So the body is one thing, and a *Sam* that develops over time is another thing. Right?

But—the body and *Sam* are not the same thing.

That's big!

So, the body and the *Sam* are not the same thing.

Sound about right so far?

Yes? Terrific.

But when that baby was born, the well-meaning conspiracy to create a *Sam* began within moments.

First the baby gets a birth certificate with the name *Sam* on it, and *immediately* everybody says *Sam, Sam, Sam* about everything that's happening around this new human.

And then—suddenly—at around two years old, that baby realizes that all those people saying *Sam* all the time are talking about their little body that's part of the experiencing going on and everything that little body does.

All at once, *Sam* seems separate; the baby is no longer an *undifferentiated* consciousness, but is now a *differentiated* consciousness called *Sam*.

Does that still sound about right?

Still yes? Great.

But this differentiated consciousness we call *Sam* doesn't just *think* it's having a unique locational experiencing of living that's part of a greater whole (that would be an integrated consciousness); the differentiation makes it suddenly *seem like* there's a *Sam* in control of the experiencing that occurs through that body.

And why wouldn't it? That little meat suit we call *Sam* gets told what to do and what not to do. Some of those patterns become conditioned behavior for that body. Those patterns become, "Just the way *Sam* is."

Little *Sam* feels like, because it *seems like*, there's a *Sam* making conscious decisions that create patterns of behavior.

Sam is treated like it's the driver of all the experiencing that goes on. Much like the driver of a car, *Sam* is treated like the one steering the separate experiencing of living down the road of life.

The body grows predictable patterns of behavior and predictable patterns of interpreting the world, and wakes up every day with mostly these same patterns. These patterns become familiar and make it *seem like* there's a *Sam* governing our unique experiencing of living.

Now, as an adult, it still seems like there's a *Sam* steering the unique experiencing of living in that location. The *seems to be* a steering *Sam* is not in doubt. But have you ever actually *looked* for a *Sam*?

To be clear, we wouldn't be looking for a body; we're not questioning whether or not there's a body with all its reactions and behavioral patterns.

Everybody can see the body, but it would be interesting to see if we can find an actual *Sam*. Especially since *Sam* is generally assumed to be running the show of this experiencing we call *Sam's life*.

Let's have a look . . . a *really* good look . . .

Step 5: Searching For an Imaginary You

The exercise that follows is a vehicle, an instrument, to drive you into the experiencing of the present moment without the distorting lens of an *Imaginary You*. It is an *experiential assist* to get you to experience the present moment as what you are. If it were a tool, it would be an experiential eraser.

The trick for the seeker is to understand that this exercise is not an attempt to conceptually prove that there is no *Imaginary You*. Instead, it is intended to provide a present moment experiencing where you can *simply notice* the utter failure in being able to find an *Imaginary You*.

By now, you know that your spiritual journey is not conceptual. It's a journey of noticing your present moment experiencing.

It's a bit of an ironic twist that your spiritual success lies in experiencing your failure to be able to find an *Imaginary You*, a believed in thought that evaporates when investigated. The distorting lens of the *Imaginary You* dissolves through the experiencing that you can't find it. All you have to do is notice.

So, stay focused on the experiencing as best you can.

Ready? Let's go...

. . .

TAKE a moment to focus your attention on your right hand. Look at the back of your hand, all the way from the wrist to the tips of the fingers. Now turn it over and look at the front of your hand from your wrist to your fingertips. Notice that this meat hand is made of skin and bones, muscles and fascia, tendons and ligaments, blood and other fluids.

Open and close your hand. Can you feel all those muscles and bones, tendons and ligaments, flexing and releasing to make that hand made of meat move?

Yes? Good.

Really focus your attention and scan that meat hand like your eyes are an infrared scanner and tell me, can you find a *Sam* anywhere in that meat hand?

No. You can't.

Right?

Don't worry; *no* one can find a *Sam* in their meat hand.

Now, do the same with that right forearm from your elbow to your wrist. Turn your wrist back and forth and watch the forearm move. Feel the sensation of it moving. Now give that meat forearm a scan and tell me, can you find a *Sam* in that meat forearm?

No. You can't.

Right?

That's okay. Nobody ever can.

Move your focus to your right upper arm. Bend and open your elbow so you can feel your biceps and triceps move. Now give that meat upper arm a good scan and tell me, can you find a *Sam* in there?

Nope. You can't find a *Sam* in that upper arm, right? No one ever does.

Now that you've got a feel for what we're doing, look at your left meat hand, left meat forearm, and left meat upper arm. Open and close your hand while you look at it. Twist your wrist back and forth; watch and feel your meat forearm move. Open and close your elbow, watch and feel your upper arm working. Experience the whole left hand and arm working.

Scan your left meat hand, left meat forearm, and left meat upper arm from fingertips to shoulder. Can you find a *Sam* in there anywhere?

No. You can't. Agreed? Nobody ever can.

And now that you know what we're doing, look at and move your right meat foot. Bend your ankle forward and back so you can see and feel your right, made of meat, lower leg work. Bend your knee so you can feel and see your upper meat leg working. Experience the entire right meat foot and leg.

Now scan the entire right meat foot and leg, top to bottom, with your full awareness and tell me if you can find a *Sam* in there.

Can you find a *Sam* in that right meat foot and leg anywhere? No, you can't. Correct?

Now repeat the whole process with your left meat foot and leg. Move them, look at them, and feel them move. Then scan the entire left meat foot and leg.

Can you find a *Sam* in the left meat foot and leg? No, you can't.

Right?

Next up, pelvis and torso . . .

Take a moment to flex your hip muscles a bit, so you can feel your pelvis move. Now, scan it to see you if you can find a *Sam* in your pelvis. Can you find a *Sam* in there?

Onto your abdomen and torso; take a couple of deep breaths so you can feel your chest and abdomen expand and contract. Now scan your chest and abdomen. Can you find a *Sam* hiding anywhere in there?

You probably didn't find a *Sam* in your pelvis, abdomen, or chest—*but*—if it *seems like* there's a *Sam* anywhere in those areas, let's take a closer look.

Wherever you feel a *Sam* may seem to be, get very specific about its location; right side, left side, up a bit, down a bit; you want to get very clear so you can point to it. Then turn all your attention on that specific area and give it a good, long, thorough scan of where in this meat body there seems to be this *Sam* person.

What happens when you investigate the specific area where there seems to be a *Sam*?

There's no *Sam* there, right? And even the *seems to be* a *Sam* disappears when you really look for it. It's rather amazing!

Seems like doesn't *make it so* is the lesson here. Sometimes *seems to be* is just that; an idea and nothing more.

Let's continue scanning as we look for a *Sam*. Take as much time as you need and focus your attention on the neck . . . any *Sam* to be found in the meat of the neck?

Probably not, but if there *seems to be* a *Sam*, then investigate. Turn all of your attention to where a Sam *seems to be*, and you'll find there's actually no *Sam* there at all when you look.

And now command central; the head. Take as much time as you'd like and scan the entire area above the neck. Tell me if you can find a *Sam* anywhere in there.

So, can you find a *Sam* up there? Probably not, but if there *seems to be* a *Sam*, then investigate. Turn all of your attention to where a *Sam seems to be*, and you'll find there's no *Sam* to be found when you try to find one. Right?

It's quite common for it to *seem like* a *Sam* in the head, especially in the brain. It's the most popular place for the feeling of *seems to be* a Sam. And yet when you focus your attention on the spot where there *seems to be* a *Sam*, it turns out that there's never one there.

I'm guessing you didn't find a *Sam*, right? It's okay; nobody else ever does either. There are a lot of *seems to be* a *Sam* moments and locations, but once they're investigated, it always turns out there was no actual *Sam* there, just a *seems like* or a *seems to be*.

Step 6 - Experiencing Continues

So, this *seems to be* you, this *Imaginary You*, couldn't be found. Agreed?

After a thorough investigation, the *Imaginary You* that seemed so real, only turned out to be a *seems like* a real you, right?

It's a very convincing *seems like*, no doubt about it, but in the end it's only a *seems to be*. Right again?

But can you notice that in the absence of an *Imaginary You* the experiencing continues uninterrupted. Yes?

Take a few minutes to look at your surroundings—notice that all experiencing continues—is that true?

Now take a moment and feel your body sensations. Breathe in and out; open and close your hands. All of the experiencing is continuing without an *Imaginary You*, right?

Notice all of the thoughts coming and going in your experiencing. Thoughts continue even without an *Imaginary You*. True?

And now for the big questions. Take your time with these and enjoy the recognition they bring about.

In the absence of an *Imaginary You*, a *Sam*, to be found anywhere—and with the awareness that *you* are still experiencing the present moment anyway—is there any doubt that what you *actually are* is the very *experiencing* of the present moment itself? That's all that's left, right?

In the absence of an *Imaginary You* . . .
If you consciously drop into your experiencing
of the present moment *experientially* . . .
Is there anything else you could *possibly* be
other than the *experiencing* itself?

After all, there's no *Imaginary You*. We looked.

Is there any way you are anything other than the pure experiencing of the present moment when that's all that's left after seeing through the *Imaginary You*?

These are important questions that most seekers never get to, despite all their earnest efforts. If the seeker has never experientially recognized that their false self only *seems to be* real, then this question can't be asked from a place of experiential recognition.

But you've done the investigation into the *Imaginary You* and come up empty. And through your own experiencing, you're left with the experiencing of the present moment as *what* you *are*. Yes?

With no *Imaginary You*, no *seems to be* a *Sam* to be found anywhere, all that's left is you *as* the experiencing. Right?

Take a moment to marinate in this realization. Most seekers will go their entire lives without ever experiencing what they are at this level.

Realizing that what you are *is* the *experiencing* of the *present moment*, is a massive shift in awareness for any human being.

In the absence of an *Imaginary You* . . . look around for a moment and just notice . . . that the *looking* is what *you are*.

Listen for a moment . . . that *listening* is what *you are*.

Feel the sensations in your body for a moment . . . that active *feeling* is what *you are*.

Notice perceptions at any level . . . the *perceiving* itself is what *you are*.

In the absence of an *Imaginary You*, you are the *perceiving*; not the *perceiver*.

Step 7: Part of a Greater Whole

Wow, so there's no *Imaginary You* to be found despite all of our looking. Just like there *seemed to be* an Imaginary Gary running the show for so many years in this location, your *Imaginary You* was just an imaginary friend too.

Every once in a while someone will ask me in casual conversation, "Did you ever have an imaginary friend as a child?" In my mind, I always chuckle and say to myself, "Not just as a child. Imaginary Gary was with me until I was 39 years old!"

Most humans go their entire lives with an imaginary friend that they believe governs all their decision making and experiencing in life. You've now seen through it; most never will.

There's no little *Imaginary You* somewhere in your head running things. And now you have an experiential understanding that it's true; not because you intellectually thought about it, but because you had the experience of looking for it and not finding it.

My previous book, *From Here To Here, Turning Toward Enlightenment*, goes into all the brain anatomy and brain functions that makes it *seem like* you're making decisions, when in fact decisions are made preconsciously, and you then become conscious of them later.

As a seeker, you just need to know experientially that the *Imaginary You* is only a *seems to be*.

You merely need to recognize that, "You're not what you're not." You're not what *seems to be* but *is not*.

Then you're left *as* the experiencing that's going on in any given moment. And this is true for everyone, all the time; whether they consciously recognize it or not.

Every person on the planet has thoughts, feelings, sights, smells, and sounds they are constantly experiencing. All of those people can report all sorts of unique experiencings. And while I won't vouch for the actuality of what they claim to be experiencing, the evidence is pretty clear that there's experiencing of some kind going on.

It's pretty clear that everyone is having their own unique experiencing in each moment, just like you are. Yes?

It's also pretty clear that others may experience the world through the lens of an illusionary separate self, but in reality, what they are *is* the *experiencing* itself. Yes again?

This means that your experiencing of living is part of a greater whole. Your experiencing is part of a larger experiencing that's going on with every person and, I would assume, with every other sentient being. Still a yes?

We could assign this *greater whole of experiencing* any label we want, but I like the term *Oneness*. The Oneness of experiencing which your unique location of experiencing is a part of, seems wonderfully simple to me.

Oneness doesn't give your conceptualizing mind too much to grab onto, but gets the point across that an *Imaginary You* doesn't control your experiencing. It elegantly expresses that this manifestation is more than just your unique location of experiencing.

"What's the purpose of this Oneness?" some may ask. Well, that's a question that a non-existent, seemingly separate, Imaginary Gary would have asked. Nobody knows the purpose of Oneness, any more than a tree knows the purpose of a forest, or a wave knows the purpose of the ocean.

I do know there's experiencing that occurs in this location of Oneness. And all evidence points to experiencing going on with all other sentient beings in their locations of Oneness as well.

And again, I'm not here to judge the *actuality* of what they claim to be experiencing, but it seems to be pretty clear that there *is* experiencing going on in those other locations.

So your unique experiencing of the greater whole in your location, and everyone else's in theirs, is what we're labeling *Oneness*.

So, in the absence of an *Imaginary You . . .*
You are left *as* the *experiencing* of the *present moment . . .*
And with the *awareness* that *others* are also the
experiencing of their locations in the *present moment . . .*
It makes *all* of our *experiencings . . .*
Part of a *greater whole.*

THIS MIGHT HAVE BEEN what the Buddha was pointing toward when he said:

Everything is One, and only the One is.

Yes?

You also may have noticed that most of the mystics and sages throughout the ages have tended to agree that we're all part of a greater whole; a Oneness.

Yes again?

And the teachings of *Non-Duality* are crystal clear on this concept of *Oneness; non-dual* literally means *not two.* The experiencing of non-separate consciousness is what non-duality points toward. So experiencing Oneness is not just implied, but stated in the actual label, *non-duality.*

Still yes?

So Let Me Ask You This...

We've looked for a *seems to be* you, an *Imaginary You*, right?

And it turns out there's no *seems to be* you, no *Imaginary You*, and there never was. *Imaginary You* seemed real enough, as did Imaginary Gary for almost 40 years. But when I experientially investigated that, it turned out that he was just an imaginary friend I'd mistakenly considered to be *me*.

Your *Imaginary You* was just an imaginary friend that you had mistakenly considered your *Self* to be.

So here we both sit. I've done a tooth to tail, nose to toes search for a Gary many, many, many, many times, and there just isn't one. I've looked. And you've done the same on your end?

Alright then, so here's the big question; and I do mean the *BIG* question—so take your time before answering it.

If your experiencing is part of a greater whole that we're calling Oneness—and there *is* only Oneness—is there any way *you* are not Oneness?

Seriously, is there any way you're not *already* Oneness, if Oneness is the *one* thing, the *only* thing, that's going on?

You *have* to be Oneness, *right*?

Now brace yourself for this one; I'll do it with you.

If your experiencing is a part of a greater whole that we call *Oneness*, which of the following is most likely to be true:

> A. I'm a separate, non-existent, *Imaginary You* that's trying to someday, in some way, discover *Oneness*.
> Or...
> B. I'm already the experiencing of *Oneness* that sometimes likes to play around at being an *Imaginary You*.

Which is it? A or B?

I want you to feel into this last question and the immensity of the answer for the spiritual seeker. When you *get* this experientially, even briefly, it will change your spiritual seeking forever.

Let's do it together. Let's see if you can feel the difference.

First, try on option A:

Am I a separate, non-existent, Imaginary Gary that's trying to someday, in some way, discover Oneness?

We've come so far by now that this question fits me like my light blue polyester leisure suit from 1973. It just feels a bit silly. If there's no actual Gary, how can a non-existent Gary discover Oneness? Oh . . . wait . . .

he can't. Wow, Imaginary Gary would probably be a little embarrassed about this if he actually existed. Good thing he doesn't . . .

Now let's try on option B:

Am I already Oneness that likes to play around at being a Gary?

Wow, I'm utterly free as Oneness that likes to play around at being a Gary. It's all Oneness and only Oneness. Even when it doesn't *seem like* it's Oneness, it's still Oneness playing around at experiencing Oneness. Even when it seems like a Gary is really doing stuff, it's still Oneness. Oh . . . my . . . gods! What a relief.

So, now let's ask ourselves another question:

In terms of our experiencing, if there's Oneness and only Oneness playing around within Oneness, is there anything else that I could ever be?

From this location of experiencing Oneness (a location that people like to call a *Gary*), all I can ever be is Oneness experiencing Oneness. Right?

How about you in your location of Oneness? Can you be anything other than Oneness playing within Oneness? Even when it's Oneness playing around at being an *Imaginary You*, aren't you still really just *Oneness*?

Hmmm, maybe the Buddha had it right all along:

Everything is One, and only the One is.

Everything is Oneness; even *you* are only ever *Oneness*.

So let me ask you this; "Who's reading this book right now?"

Well, you've seen through your imaginary self, so it's not the *Imaginary You*, right?

This location of experiencing, this location of experiencing that's part of a greater whole, is what we're labeling Oneness. So it must be Oneness reading this book right now. Right again?

There's only a *seems to be Imaginary You*—no actual, separate *You*. You'll recall that we looked for an actual you, but couldn't find one, so it must be Oneness reading these words. Yes?

The Spiritual Seeker's Journey

Most seekers begin their spiritual journey believing themselves to be a self that, it turns out, is actually imaginary. They've been conditioned to believe they're a *Sam*, or a *Mary*, or a *Gary*, or a *Joan* their entire lives. So naturally, they begin their journey by trying to find ways to *wake up* their imaginary selves.

I know I sure did. I started by trying to gradually improve Imaginary Gary in hopes that one-day Imaginary Gary would, "Awaken to the experiencing of Oneness."

But let me ask you this . . .

How long do you think it would take to *wake up* an Imaginary Gary? How long would it take to *wake up* a self that doesn't actually exist?

That would be, "What is *forever*, Alex, for a thousand." And the judges would say, "That's correct!" But since trying to wake something up that doesn't exist will never happen, I personally think it would take even *longer* than forever.

Make sense?

Seriously, think about this dilemma that you've just seen through, one that most spiritual seeker's never will. It's why most seekers go their entire lives without having an experiencing of Oneness. If they can't experientially see through the illusion of the nonexistent, imaginary self they believe themselves to be, then the spiritual seeking will go on forever.

Trust me, this is not meant as criticism. I've been there myself. I'm just pointing out the suffering for the seeker.

And for those seekers who have at least intellectually seen through the illusion of the imaginary self, things can still get slippery. They will often, unknowingly, continue seeking as if a nonexistent, imaginary self is going to wake up a nonexistent, imaginary self to the fact that a nonexistent, imaginary self doesn't exist.

Phewwwwww! Try doing that for a decade or two and see how exhausted you get.

This is where the seekers will say (I said it too), "I understand all of this intellectually, but I'm just not having the experience."

The truth is that you're *always* having *the experience*; you just don't understand it intellectually. That's because you *can't* understand it intellectually *until* you've understood it experientially.

Generally, the seeker has it all backwards—until suddenly—they don't.

Once you experientially get that there's no *Imaginary You*, and that your unique experiencing of living is part of a greater whole of experiencing that we're calling *Oneness*, then you're left being the continual present moment experiencing of Oneness in your location.

Oneness doesn't mean *sameness*, but your unique locational experiencing of Oneness is still Oneness—period—a wave in the ocean is still a part of the ocean.

There's no Imaginary Gary, Imaginary Sam, or Imaginary You that's controlling your experience as an experiencer, so that leaves you *as* the *experiencing*.

Now Those Ancient Pointings Make Sense

So, let's see what this new experiential understanding is like with a few classic non-dual pointings.

I am, but there is no me.

Take a moment and shift back to the way most spiritual seekers are experiencing living. Step back into the illusion of a separate, *Imaginary You* that falsely believes they're in control of their experiencing. From that false place of experiencing, try to interpret this pointing:

I am, but there is no me.

I am. Okay, that makes sense to a degree. There is a sense of being. However, if you believe you're a separate *Imaginary You* out there trying to discover Oneness, then how does *there is no ME* make any sense at all?

From the point of view of an *Imaginary You*, *I am* and *me* are the same thing. As an imaginary, separate self I will thirst for more concepts to explain this pointing, and the concepts will only add to my illusion of separateness. I'll be drinking saltwater trying to quench my thirst.

Now, take a moment and investigate again—*really* investigate—to see if you can find an *Imaginary You*.

Take as long as you'd like, but have the experiencing of looking for an *Imaginary You* in your body and not finding one. I'll wait.

Did you do it? Good.

So, we both know that it often *seems like* there's an *Imaginary You*, but when you investigate, you can't find one. In the absence of finding an *Imaginary You*, you now have the actual present moment experiencing of the absence of an *Imaginary You*.

In the absence of an *Imaginary You*, you're left *as* the *experiencing* of the *present moment* from your *unique* locational *Oneness*.

Suddenly, *I am* as the experiencing of Oneness in this location makes perfect sense, both experientially and conceptually. And, *but there is no ME*, makes perfect sense both experientially and conceptually—*because* you're in a place of *experiencing* this actuality, not just *thinking* about it—you looked for a *ME* and couldn't find one.

Let's look at another classic non-dual pointer:

You are the perceiving, not the perceiver.

Take a moment and drop into that *seems to be* a self we call *Imaginary You*. Buy into the illusion that most of humanity will never question, which is that what you are is a separate, independent self.

Now look around at your current surroundings and notice that when you identify as the *Imaginary You*, you seem like a separate perceiver, and whatever is perceived appears as separate, external objects. There's an *Imaginary You* as perceiver, and a separate object that is perceived.

Now take a moment and investigate, again, to see if you can find the *Imaginary You*. Have the experiencing of not finding the *Imaginary You* that seems so real. Go ahead. I'll wait.

Did you do it? Great.

In the absence of an *Imaginary You*, what you are *is* the present moment experiencing. In the absence of a separate self, there's *only* experiencing. There is no separate perceiver, and no separately perceived objects. There is only present moment perceiving.

You know experientially there's only perceiving, so the concept in the pointing is clear. But without experiencing the absence of the separate self, the seeker can't ever fully grasp what the pointing is truly pointing toward.

Let's try this one on for size:

You are already enlightened. You just don't know it.

Imagine now that you're a separate *Imaginary You*, who's seeking a thing called *enlightenment*. You think, believe, and experience the world as a separate being, so how on earth could this *Imaginary You* already be enlightened?

Now experientially investigate and see if you can find the *Imaginary You* that *wants to be enlightened*. Go ahead, take a good look.

Did you do the investigation? Good job.

With no one who wants to be enlightened (*Imaginary You*) to be found, you're left *as* the flow of experiencing in the continual *this-here-now*. With no *Imaginary You* creating the illusion of separateness, *you* are *always already enlightened* because that's all you've ever been.

I vividly remember the first time I heard this pointing. Decades ago, I was eating lunch at an outdoor cafe on California Avenue in Palo Alto, California. My friend quoted his guru who had said, "You're already enlightened. You just don't know it."

"Well, thanks for nothing. That doesn't help," I replied.

How would an Imaginary Gary ever get that pointer? Only after realizing that Imaginary Gary didn't exist was I able to see that everyone *was* already enlightened. But let's be clear; it's a different *You* that's already enlightened. A *Gary* never gets to be enlightened. A *Joan* or a *Sam* never gets to be enlightened. It's the *absence* of a Gary, a Joan, or a Sam that's already enlightened.

When you're grounded in the experiencing of non-separate, non-dual consciousness, all these classic pointings make sense because those that spoke them were speaking from the experiential side of the gateless gate.

The game is to get experientially grounded in the absence of an *Imaginary You*, so you're left as the *Oneness* you always already are. Then all the spiritual teachings suddenly make sense.

Once you know the *play*book, the game becomes quite simple.

Summary

We've just gone through a whole sequence of questions, noticings, and all out investigations, to funnel you down into the experiencing of the present moment *as* what you are.

By seeing through the *Imaginary You*, the vacuum seal on the illusion of a separate *You* as the experiencer who's in charge of their experiencing in a separately experienced world, has been broken.

By recognizing your unique experiencing as part of a

greater whole of experiencing, the arrow of experiencing is reversed. You can relax into the *experiencing as Oneness* in your location. There's no longer an *Imaginary You* trying to be *in charge*.

You're a unique expression of Oneness (*not* sameness) that occasionally plays around at experiencing itself as an *Imaginary You*, but is always still Oneness playing within Oneness to experience Oneness.

For most of you, this will be the first time this has ever occurred. For others, there may have been similar experiencings of this somewhere in the past. Either way, what's essential is that you now have a reference point for a present moment experiencing without the disorienting filter of a nonexistent *Imaginary You* in the way.

You've had the *One Taste*; a conscious taste of present moment experiencing *as what you are*. This is an experiencing that most seekers will never have.

And the shocking simplicity of it is that you're the active experiencing of each present moment, whatever that experiencing may be, and this has always been the case.

That's it. This is it. You're not a noun; a *doer*. You're the verb *being*; the verb of *experiencing*.

Take a moment and feel the stunning effortlessness of not being an imagined *doer*, and instead being the magnificent and unique experiencing of each moment —*continually*. Sit with that for a bit . . .

Truth be told, you only need one concept to be experientialized for the process of awakening to occur; and that's the concept of an illusionary self. I refer to it as the *Imaginary You*. Others refer to it as *The False Self*, *The ME*, *The Persona*, etc. The seeing through of this *Imaginary You* at an experiential level breaks the illusion of separateness.

In the absence of an *Imaginary You*, and with no valid evidence of an *Imaginary You* actually existing, you're left as only experiencing itself.

The bonus concept is that of *Oneness*, which is that your experiencing is part of a greater whole.

With the simple noticing of the unique experiencing of others going on all around you, your experiencing becomes quite obviously part of a greater whole.

As Oneness *the arrow of experiencing is reversed* and the experiencing of yourself as *the unique present moment experiencing of Oneness in your location* occurs. Not *sameness*, but an absolutely *unique*, locational experiencing of Oneness.

Here's a summary example of the soft-style PMI experiencing we just went through:

- Who *seems* to be having this experience?

- Can I find them if I look for them? (Actually look for them in the body.)

- In the absence of the *seems to be* a self, in the absence of the *Imaginary You*, does experiencing in your location continue?

- In the absence of an *Imaginary You*, is there *any* way you are *not* left *as* the *experiencing* of the *present moment* in *your location*?

- With the awareness of others having their own unique experiencings of the present moment in their locations, is there any way your experiencing is not part of a greater whole of experiencing going on?

- If we label the greater whole of experiencing *Oneness*, is there any way you're *not* the unique experiencing of Oneness in your location?

- As you're consciously aware of being Oneness playing within Oneness to experience Oneness in your location, what's it like to be the experiencing Oneness in each present moment?

Now, let's uncover how you might abide in this awakening, shall we?

4

GROWING THE ONE TASTE

Once You Get It, You've Got It

WE COULD HAVE A PIANO TEACHER COME TO YOUR location right now and play you some examples of *dissonance* and *consonance*. And even if you're someone utterly untrained in music, in well under two minutes, you'd *get it*. You'd be able to feel the difference because you would have had a present moment experiencing of dissonance and consonance.

Consonance would sound kind of smooth, pleasant, and enjoyable. Dissonance would feel somewhat tense, unpleasant, or even harsh. You'd feel pretty confident that you had this *dissonance* versus *consonance* stuff down; and rightly so.

Your teacher would be able to play random examples of notes, chords, or intervals, and without even knowing what those things are, you'd be able to call them out as consonant or dissonant with a fair degree of accuracy. You'd just dip into your experiencing from your short lesson, and the answers would be obvious.

But if for some reason the music gods and goddesses wished to torment you, you'd next be escorted into a nearby room full of musicians who had studied music theory . . . a *lot* of music theory. There you would toss out the simple question, "Can anyone explain what dissonance and consonance are in music?"

You would then have to jump back, because the explosion of concepts unleashed by the group would be nothing short of spectacular. People would begin speaking about majors and minors, perfect and diminished fifths, tri-tones, ratios, and square roots of things (!), Debussy, and even the "devil's tone".

Uff da!

Luckily, before you ran into this hailstorm of concepts about dissonance and consonance, you were already grounded in the experiencing of them. But now, you'll find yourself questioning what you truly know. Too many concepts can do that to a person. They can drive you batty.

The good news is, that no matter how confused you become, you'll have an experiential reference point for dissonance and consonance. We could bring you right back over to the piano, and you'd be able to easily tell someone whether something being played was dissonant or consonant.

It's no different with a conscious awakening. Once you've been the experiencing of it, you know what it is experientially. You no longer need any concepts.

Since you've been there, you can revisit being the experiencing of the present moment *as what you are* again, and again, and again. Since the experiencing of the present moment is always what you are, there's only ever the recognition of what is already the case. And that's all that's left for you to do.

We're going to show you how to find that experiential present moment *place* of awakening, as often as you're so inclined to find it. You'll be able to revisit often, so it can grow in your everyday experiencing. Eventually, you can have the *One Taste* abide *as* your everyday experiencing.

Much like noticing the difference between dissonance and consonance, the game now is just to notice the difference between the present moment experienced as an imaginary, separate self, versus the experiencing of the present moment *as* what *you are*, as *Oneness*. No big concepts required.

When you do notice your experiencing is occurring through the lens of an illusionary, separate self, you can just investigate the present moment to see if you can find this seemingly real *Imaginary You*. And when the *Imaginary You* is nowhere to be found (yet again), you'll be left as the experiencing of the present moment *as* what you *are*.

You already *get it*. Now we just have to let it take root and grow in your experienicing.

Growing the One Taste With PMI

The first experiencing of non-dual consciousness, of experiencing the present moment *as* what you *are*, is called an *awakening*. It's the *One Taste*.

The first purpose of Present Moment Investigation (PMI) is to steer you into the One Taste. The second purpose of PMI is to grow the One Taste from an unstable, occasional happening into a place of abidance.

Shen Hui said,

There is a difference between Awakening and deliverance. The former is sudden, but thereafter deliverance is gradual.

Deliverance, or as I say, *abidance*, is gradual in the sense that it most often takes some time to unwind the habit of viewing the present moment through the lens of an *Imaginary You*. It's PMI that unwinds the habit of an *Imaginary You* better than anything else I know of.

After all, once you've seen through the *Imaginary You*, it gets more and more difficult to take your false self too seriously. "Investigate and marinate" is the motto. That's all that's left to do. Investigate the present moment and then marinate in the experiencing of the present moment *as* what you *are*.

It's important to understand that PMI is not attempting to change *what is*. The intention of PMI is to *recognize* what *actually* is.

Quite often, it's the *Imaginary You* that seems to be an independent, separate self that desires for *what actually is* to be different. And that's all fine, because when we investigate, we find that the *Imaginary You* was just a believed in thought anyway.

That leaves you left to marinate *as* the *experiencing* of the present moment, whatever that may contain.

PMI is just an attempt to discover more intimately what's going on *now*. It drives you more deeply into present moment experiencing; it *doesn't* try to *change* it.

In the soft-style martial art of Tai Chi Chuan, there's a well-known exercise called *Sticky Hands*. With your hand on top of the hand of your training partner, you just follow their movements wherever they may go, with no resistance and no expectations.

In some ways, PMI is just *sticky experiencing* as you investigate and find whatever it is you happen to find. You experience whatever it is you experience with no expectations.

It's only the *Imaginary You* that gets in the way of you experiencing each present moment *as* the experiencing itself. It's the attachment an *Imaginary You* has to things being some other way than the way they are that keeps things from *sticking*.

It's our resistance to things being *as they are* that gets in the way of our experiencing each present moment *as* what *we are*. And what is it that creates the resistance? None other than the *Imaginary You*, of course.

So, the game with PMI is to investigate whatever *is* in the *moment*. If there happens to be attachment, investigate, "*Who is attached*?" If there happens to be resistance, investigate, "*Who is resisting*?"

PMI investigates whatever is going on in the present moment with no expectations. That's true even if you're investigating, "*Who is having these expectations*?"

The PMI goes the way it goes. Whichever way it goes, that's the way it goes.

But each time you re-awaken to the experiencing of the present moment as what you are, the PMI is growing the One Taste. You go from a first awakening, to occasional awakening, to frequent awakening, to an abiding experiencing of the present moment as what you are.

Repetition Is Key

You have now seen through the *Imaginary You*, the imaginary doer. The common question that follows is, "If there's no doer, how can there be anything to do?"

Although it's true there's no doer, there absolutely are things to be done to eventually abide in the experiencing of the present moment *as* what you *are*. This is often confusing to seekers, but it's not much different than what goes on in the rest of our day to day living.

There's no doer, but things in our lives get done all the time. There's no doer, but when hunger occurs in your location of experiencing, eating gets done. When your car is low on gasoline, there's no doer, but filling the gas tank gets done. Things get done constantly, despite the fact that there's no doer.

PMI is no different. There's no doer, but when interest in investigating the present moment arises, a Present Moment Investigation gets done.

There's no doer, but as PMI gets done regularly, the growing experiencing of the One Taste, the experiencing of Oneness as what you are, gets done. It's no different than watering a seed getting done so a plant grows.

It's not complicated. Things get done all the time, despite there being no doer. PMI is no different.

The PMI Secret Ingredients

I've always been a bit envious of polyglots—there's no reason for me to lie about it—it's been true since the eighth grade. For a long time, I thought it was just me; I've since realized I may have been wrong.

Personal experience has shown me that *polyglot envy* is a common occurrence. Those folks who speak multiple languages, known as *polyglots*, have always seemed to be in on some kind of secret that I wasn't privy to when it came to learning languages. Those in the polyglot club would share what they knew, but I still couldn't figure it out for myself.

As it turns out, they *do* have a secret. Researchers have discovered that polyglots can learn new languages so rapidly because they use a radical approach that's often missed by others.

What polyglots do that others don't is to figure out ways of learning that they actually enjoy, and then employ those methods consistently over time through repetition. The methods vary a great deal among poly-glots, but the common denominator is enjoyment, pleasure, and even fun.

I'd venture to say that those who approach awakening like a polyglot approaches learning a new language are onto something big . . . very big indeed.

While there's no doer to make anything in particular

happen, it would probably be nice to know the secret ingredients that make up the superfood for growing the *One Taste* of conscious awakening. If adding the following flavors to your PMI happens, then it will only make your PMI's that much more powerful.

Let's look at some secret ingredients.

A Playful Attitude

I can't emphasize enough how beneficial a playful attitude is when doing your PMI. When it naturally happens during your investigations, everything tends to go better.

A PLAYFUL ATTITUDE comes more naturally to some than to others, so don't force it. However, if you notice that your PMI is more effective when you're playful with it, those seeds will tend to grow.

When your PMI becomes *play* rather than *practice*, you'll know you're on the right track.

A Calm Desire for the Truth

Much like a detective must have a calm desire to follow the evidence wherever it leads, this is also essential when you're doing PMI. As you investigate to find an *Imaginary You*, a, "Let the chips fall where they may," attitude makes it much more effective.

A DESIRE for things to go a certain way is a sure sign that the *Imaginary You* has hijacked your PMI. It's not a big deal since that too is just *what is*. But when the *Imaginary You* hijacks your PMI, it's less likely to drop you into an experiencing of the present moment as what you are.

Curiosity

A genuine curiosity about the miraculous *experiencing* of living is a big plus for your PMI. If you can step back occasionally and take note of how fascinating your investigation into the nature of personal reality actually is, it won't be hard to remain curious.

I WAS ALWAYS CONSTANTLY curious about how an Imaginary Gary could *seem to be* so real, and yet could never be found in my current location when I actually looked for him. And I was just as curious about the fact that no one was ever in anyone else's location when they looked either.

"Curiouser and curiouser," expressed the Cheshire Cat in *Alice in Wonderland*. In some ways, the cat summed it up well. This experiencing of living is just wonderfully curiouser and curiouser.

Optimism

Optimism is a sure sign that your PMI is being done well. Ideally, whatever present moment experiencing that you investigate, there should be an authentic search for whomever it is that *seems to be* having a separate experience.

WHEN I USED to do PMI regularly, I optimistically searched for an Imaginary Gary each time. Why wouldn't I? Imaginary Gary *seemed to be* as real as could be; until I actually searched and couldn't find him.

I was like the optimist in an old joke about twins. As it goes, one twin was a perpetual pessimist, and one twin was an eternal optimist. The parents thought it would be good if each had a chance to experience the other's reality. So, on their birthday, they gave the pessimist twin the most spectacular toy firetruck ever built, and they gave the optimist twin a big box full of horse manure.

Sure enough, when the twins opened their presents, the pessimistic twin immediately began complaining because the firetruck didn't shoot water or have a real engine. But unexpectedly, the optimistic twin began gleefully running through the house. When the parents asked the optimist why he was so happy, he said, "With that much horse poop, there's got to be a pony around here somewhere!"

I was always the optimist in my PMI. With so much Imaginary Gary manure around, with so much *seems to be* an actual Gary in my experiencing, there just had to be a Gary around there somewhere. There never was, of course—not even once—and no pony either, by the way . . .

Amusement

A sense of humor is the ultimate secret weapon for the spiritual seeker. And it was one of the major by-products of most of my PMI's. I would optimistically investigate to see if I could find a Gary. The *seems to be* a Gary was so close there just had to be one. How could it have only been a *seems like* a Gary my entire life?

AND THEN MY INVESTIGATION WOULD, yet again, come up empty handed . . . no Gary to be found anywhere, despite the persistent *seems to be* a Gary.

How could I not find that wonderfully amusing? It truly is the biggest joke going. And once you learn to be amused, the game only gets better.

Positive Emotion
I was always optimistic that I'd find a Gary, and instead ended up being amused when I couldn't. As I found myself to be the experiencing of the present moment, it would frequently turn into an experiencing of joy, wonder, or fascination. Not always, but quite often.

LANDING IN A PLACE of positive emotion, while certainly not required, does make the whole PMI experience more likely to be repeated. When it's consciously occurring and the inclination arises, take a moment to revel in the experiencing of the present moment as what you are.

The fact that there's experiencing occurring at all is a genuine miracle; actually, as far as miracles go, it might be the biggest one of all. That's a good thing to remember.

The Power in the Mundane Moment
A final note on the secret ingredients; don't underestimate diving into some PMI during the mundane moments of life.

SO OFTEN, PMI is used by seekers to shift out of unpleasant experiencings, commonly referred to as *suffering* in many spiritual traditions, caused by viewing the world through the lens of a separate, illusionary self. It's where most seekers begin, because suffering is a great motivator for seeking something better.

When you do PMI during ordinary, mundane moments, by asking, "Who is having this experiencing right now? Can I find them?" you can much more easily see right through the *Imaginary You.* Then it will be that much easier to be left *as* the experiencing of the present moment.

So, take advantage of PMI during those moments when *nothing's going on* and you'll grow the *One Taste* even more rapidly.

The PMI Habit

In the world of spiritual seeking there are an almost infinite number of spiritual practices to choose from. It's subtle, but most of those practices don't tend to aim at our present moment experiencing. Instead, they aim toward a *Future You* experiencing life in a different and more enjoyable way.

As you know, our present moment experiencing is *all* that's ever *actually* going on. It's the only workbench we have available, so best to use it in a way that doesn't deny the actuality of our experiencing.

Present Moment Investigation is just what the title implies; an investigation into the moment at hand to see if we can more accurately experience the *actuality* of what's going on *now*.

PMI is the most potent spiritual tool I know of because it drives you deeper into what you *always already are*; the *experiencing* of the *present moment*.

And do notice that the *I* in PMI purposely stands for *investigation*; the *I* doesn't stand for *inquiry*. The concept of *inquiry* causes many spiritual seekers to merely check in with their conceptual minds about an imaginary self—an *Imaginary You*—to make sure they remember the concept correctly.

The word *Investigation* intentionally points toward an actual, *experiential* search, and *then* an actual, *experiential* failure to find an *Imaginary You* in the present moment. An investigation means to actually search; not to just think and intellectualize about it.

One of my students asked recently, "What's the difference between thinking about investigating and investigating?"

I replied, "It's the same as the difference between thinking about looking for your lost car keys and actually getting up and looking for your car keys."

That's the difference.

The Power of PMI Is In the Soft-Style

Remember way back in Part 1 of this book when you learned that *soft-style* is generally the most powerful way to go if one wants to experientialize spiritual concepts?

Soft-styling your PMI is the key to your spiritual seeking success because it seeks no *future* success.

Soft-style PMI offers no resistance to present moment experiencing; it doesn't even resist resistance if that's present. It just investigates it. It brings with it no intention to change the present moment experiencing; it doesn't even try to change a desire to change the present moment experiencing. It just investigates it. Soft-style PMI merely aims to discover any false perceptions that distort the experiencing of the present moment *as it is.*

In another section of this book, you realized that there's no *Imaginary You* controlling the experiencing of living. You discovered that your experiencing of each moment is part of a greater whole of experiencing we've labeled *Oneness,* and that your unique experiencing *as* the present moment is *what you are.* The present moment flow of Oneness, in your location, *is* what you *are.*

If it's all Oneness and there's no *Imaginary You* that should or shouldn't remember to do or not to do PMI, then it's all up to Oneness, which you always already are. So when Oneness notices that it would like to engage in PMI in your location of Oneness, then Oneness will initiate a curiosity about the present moment and engage in PMI. It couldn't be simpler.

And if Oneness in your location *really* gets into pretending to be an *Imaginary You*, either for something wonderful *You* did, or something unpleasant *You* experienced as an imaginary, separate self, well . . . that's all up to Oneness too, so there's no separate self to criticize about not doing PMI sooner.

In this regard, PMI is not a practice. Ideally, it's more present moment *play*. PMI is a style of investigating the present moment—*soft-style*.

The PMI Confluence

Many mornings, at 4:30 am, I walk down a narrow country road in my little California town. The street has no sidewalks. It has potholes o'plenty and loose asphalt abounds.

I enjoy my walk down this road because there's very little traffic. It's mostly just me, the skunks and the coyotes at that time of day.

The country road is wide enough that I can move to the very edge of the paved road without breaking stride to let a car pass. There's virtually no traffic on the road at that time of the morning, so one would think the road, the few cars, and I would experience the bliss of unencumbered forward motion in the dark silence.

However, while it's true that there's very little traffic on my narrow country road, I'm always amused by the confluence of events that so often take place.

Most mornings I can walk for an entire hour, about 4 miles, and no more than two cars will pass me during that time. What's fascinating to me is that most often those two cars (inevitably approaching each other from different directions) and I will all come together at the same time, at the exact same point on the road.

This means that I have to step off the road into damp tree branches, mud, or even a puddle to let the cars pass each other without hitting me.

Each car had an entire hour to come down the road while I walked. If my trip or theirs were to begin even ten seconds sooner or later, the confluence of us all meeting at the same point would never happen. But it does, and fairly regularly.

It seems to happen about every other time I go out for my early morning walk. It's genuinely fascinating to me (even with one muddy, wet foot).

The same holds true for your PMI—it's just as fascinating—if you step back and consider what has to happen for you to be able to engage in PMI in the first place, it's awe inspiring.

Let's clearly define *why* it's so amazing; so awe inspiring. Most human beings *never* even *consider* that the false self they believe themselves to be is only built by their imaginations. Even most of the spiritual seekers who *intellectually* understand that they're not the false self, will never *experientially* see through their *imaginary* selves.

Most seekers will never realize themselves *as* the *experiencing* of the *present moment*. And they'll also never realize that they're the experiencing of Oneness playing within Oneness.

So, for the confluence of your experiencing of Oneness in your location to notice that it may be experiencing the moment through the false lens of an *Imaginary You* —and for Oneness to then initiate an experiential investigation to discover if there actually *is* an *Imaginary You*—is incredible.

The fact that we have present moment experiencing at all is a miracle. So, to get to the place where you're engaging in an investigation, which leads you to the recognition that what you are is the experiencing itself, is a *double* miracle. It's actually *way* beyond miraculous.

PMI Works By Just Noticing What Is

The basic PMI process in any moment is to ask, "Who seems to be having this experience?" And then actually investigate to have a present moment experiencing of the answer.

Many seekers who engage in self-inquiry will ask, "Who seems to be having this experience?" And they'll then engage their intellectual understanding of concepts and think, "Well, even though it seems like it, I know it's not the *False Self*, the *Me*, the *Ego*, because I know they don't exist. So it must be these other concepts . . . etc., etc."

Blah. No fun at all.

Intellectually, whatever concepts they come up with to describe the situation, may be on the *spiritually correct* list of *approved* non-dual concepts. And yet, those concepts will never be the actual experiencing of the present moment that occurs without the distorting lens of a nonexistent, *Imaginary You*.

And paradoxically, if you want this investigation to be most effective, then the ideal intention is to not want to change anything. The ideal intention is to try to see as clearly as possible the experiencing of the present moment for what it is. Oddly, this is when things generally change the most, because the *Imaginary You* isn't in their reinforcing itself by trying to make things different.

Who Thinks Things Shouldn't Be
Exactly The Way They Are In
This Present Moment?

SO THE BASIC set-up for a PMI is to notice when you believe that something that has already happened, "Shouldn't have happened." This is a sure sign that an *Imaginary You* is hijacking your experiencing of the present moment.

What I mean is, that believing that something that's already happened should *not* have happened because an *Imaginary You* apparently knows how everything *should* be is a big clue; that's when playing with PMI might be a good idea.

Your goal is to investigate who's actually having the experiencing of something being that shouldn't be. That's all. And let me be clear; this doesn't mean that your location of Oneness *shouldn't* initiate actions that may change things in the future. *If* that happens, that's *what is* as well.

So, your first question is, "Who seems to believe this shouldn't be the way things are?" Remember, we never call into question the *seems to be* of things, if that's what's occurring. We just want to investigate if the *seems like* is true.

In my case, the answer would be that it *seems like* there's a Gary believing that something that *already is*, shouldn't be.

Interesting! Let's investigate and see if that's true.

Can we find a Gary who believes this thought when we actually look for him?

Well, let's do a quick experiential scan of the meat suit that this Gary guy seems to inhabit. Can we find a Gary?

Doing a quick scan (actually *doing* it, not just *thinking* about it) from the feet up to the top of the neck does not find a Gary. *But* . . . it *seems like* there might be a Gary on the right side of my brain. Let's investigate that . . .

I'll take all of the attention that's usually focused outward at the world, and turn it around to focus on the spot in my brain where just seconds ago there seemed to be a Gary. Oh, wow! Once again, when I actually look there, when I thoroughly explore that area, there's no Gary to be found.

But I looked. I actually looked. And so I had the actual experiencing of not finding a Gary. For the umpteenth time, I still found no Gary.

So, after once again not finding a Gary, the next question in our Present Moment Investigation is, "In the absence of a Gary, what am I? What am I left as?"

Well, as the experiencing of the present moment without a Gary, I'm left *as* the *experiencing* of the *present moment* as what *I am*.

But I'm still curious about this experiencing without an Imaginary Gary, so let's widen the investigation with some other PMI questions; soft-style, of course . . .

Is my unique experiencing the only experiencing going on in the world, or is my experiencing part of a greater whole of experiencing, since everyone else in the world is currently having their own experiencing while I'm having mine?

It's pretty clear there's other experiencing going on all around me, so my experiencing *must* be part of a greater whole of experiencing. Yes?

Let's call that wholeness of the totality of experiencing *Oneness*.

So I'm the experiencing of Oneness in this location. That's what I am. True?

There's no Imaginary Gary creating the experiencing, so it must be Oneness experiencing Oneness in this location. Right?

Ahhhhh . . . I'm the continual flow of experiencing Oneness in this location. No matter what that experiencing is, that's what I am. I'm a continual flowing of the, *What's actually happening now,* experiencing of Oneness.

My conceptual question was answered experientially. My question wasn't solved—it was dissolved.

Angry?
Anyone? Anyone? Anyone?

LET'S TAKE A RIDE TOGETHER. Imagine this along with me, and do what I do.

A double miracle occurs when you actually notice that there's an experiencing of anger in the present moment, and that you'd like to investigate it. Unlike most other spiritual practices, your goal isn't to attempt to change the current experiencing; your goal is to investigate *who* is actually *experiencing*.

Your first question is, "Who seems to be having this experiencing of anger?"

Remember, we never call into question the *seems to be* of things. If the *seems to be* of something is part of your experiencing, there's no reason to deny it. We just want to investigate if the *seems to be* is just a *seems like*, or if it's actually something more.

In my case, the answer would be that it *seems like* there's a Gary experiencing anger. Very curious, indeed. Let's investigate and see if that's true.

Can we find Gary if we actually look for him?

Well, let's do a quick experiential scan of the body that this Gary seems to inhabit. Can we find a Gary in the meat suit?

A quick scan from the feet up to the top of the neck doesn't come up with a Gary. But it *seems like* there might be a Gary directly behind my eyes, in my brain . . . Yep, there's a pretty strong *seems to be* a Gary in there. So, let's investigate that.

I'll put all of the attention that's usually focused outward at the world, and I'll turn it around and focus it on the spot in my brain where just seconds ago there *seemed to be* a Gary. Whoa! Once again, when I actually look there, there's no Gary to be found.

But I looked. I actually looked. And I had the experiencing of not finding a Gary. Again. Haha!

After once again not finding a Gary, the next question in our Present Moment Investigation is, "In the absence of a Gary, what am I?"

As the experiencing of the present moment without a Gary, I'm left as the experiencing of the present moment as what I am. I'm the flowing experiencing of the present moment itself.

But I'm still curious, so the question arises, "Is my location of experiencing the only experiencing that's going on, or is it part of a greater whole of experiencing by all other beings as well?

It's pretty clear there's other experiencing going on all around me (and a lot of it) so my experiencing must be part of a greater whole I'll call Oneness.

It appears that I'm the experiencing of Oneness in this location. That is what I am. There's no Gary creating the experiencing (we investigated and couldn't find one), so it must be Oneness. Yes?

Honestly, there was no intention to get rid of the anger, but with no imaginary, separate self that *seems to be* angry, the anger was left behind and no longer part of this present moment experiencing.

Fascinating . . .

Who Wants To Awaken?
Anyone? Anyone? Anyone?

THIS IS a question that can be profoundly insightful when investigated. So let's dive in and see what turns up.

I know spiritual seekers often have thoughts about wanting to awaken, so let me ask you, dear reader, "Who wants to awaken?"

Can we find an entity, a separate being that wants to awaken if we look?

Well, let's look. If you scan your body from the tips of your toes to the top of your head, can you find a *You* that wants to awaken? Take a moment and do a Present Moment Investigation of your meat suit made of blood and bones, and tell me if you can find a *You* that wants to awaken.

Take your time . . . I'll wait.

So what did you find? Again, I don't doubt that when the topic of awakening arises, it sure seems like there's a *You* that wants to awaken, but did you actually find a one?

No? Okay . . . so in the absence of an *Imaginary You* that wants to awaken, what remains?

The experiencing remains. Is that true?

Are you once again left *as* the experiencing of the present moment, whatever that experiencing may be?

What's that like?

It's different than experiencing the present moment through the lens of an *Imaginary You*, isn't it? Take a moment to notice the difference.

Awakening to the present moment *as* the experiencing of that present moment leaves no one left who would want to awaken, because it's already so.

Fish in the ocean don't pray for rain.

Who Doesn't Want To Suffer?
Anyone? Anyone? Anyone?

OCCASIONALLY, we all find ourselves in unpleasant situations. And it's natural in those situations to sometimes desire for suffering to end.

What if we asked of our experiencing, "Who is it that doesn't want to suffer?"

Can we find a *You* that doesn't want to suffer?

We're not just going to inquire intellectually. Let's experientially look. Let's investigate.

Take a moment to scan your entire meat suit and tell me if you can find a *You* that doesn't want to suffer.

Did you find one?

And in the absence of finding a *You* that doesn't want to suffer, what are you left as?

Are you left as the miracle of experiencing each moment *as what you are*?

Are you left *as* an experiencing that's part of a greater whole we call Oneness?

Are you thereby a locational experiencing of Oneness, regardless of what experiencing is occurring in any moment?

That's my experiencing.

What's it like in your location of experiencing Oneness?

The Subtle Power Of Softness

The secret power of PMI is its softness. It offers no *resistance*.

In the soft-style martial arts, "*If you push, I pull,*" and, "*If you pull, I push,*" is the way. If you're physically going in a certain direction, I don't try to prevent you from going in that direction; I *assist* you in going in that direction. I assist you as much as possible in experiencing where you're going, and you end up throwing yourself.

In the art of improvisational comedy, or *Improv*, the players don't resist anything that's offered to them from other players or audience members. The two key words in Improv are, "Yes, And." "Yes," I fully accept what you offered, "And," I'm going to add something to it. Ideally, they add something the audience finds funny, and everybody laughs.

With PMI, acceptance isn't needed so you can throw a body or make an audience laugh. Your acceptance of the experiencing in the moment is necessary so you can thoroughly investigate the *actuality* of your present moment experiencing.

When you investigate your present moment experiencing, you end up consciously experiencing the present moment. And since the present moment is all there ever is, you consciously awaken to the *actuality* that what you are *is* the experiencing of the present moment.

Thus, when you really get the flavor of PMI, it's quite enjoyable; it's playful. And when you *really* get the feel for PMI, you can easily begin your PMI with questions like, "Can I find the one who believes that?" or "Can I find the one who doesn't want to be separate?" etc., etc. . . .

Even figuring out the soft-style questions can be fun.

A PMI habit is a sure way to grow the *One Taste* of conscious awakening into a regular occurrence, and then into an *abidance* in who you *always already are;* the experiencing of the present moment *as what you are;* the unique, locational experiencing of Oneness, playing within Oneness experiencing Oneness.

That's it. *Being This-Here-Now* is always already it.

Summary

We began this section by talking a bit about music. Once you've had the conscious experiencing of dissonance and consonance, it's relatively easy to notice which one is occurring in any given moment.

This is very similar to the seeker who has had an experiencing of the *One Taste* after seeing through the *Imag-*

inary You. They can now notice the difference in their experiencing when it's occurring through the lens of a false self, and when it's not.

The PMI habit is just about noticing and investigating the present moment. It's not an attempt to try to change the experiencing being investigated, although the experiencing often does change. It's merely an attempt to get to the actuality of the present moment.

Each repetition of PMI grows the One Taste of the flowing experiencing of the present moment as what you are. Each time you experientially recognize that there's no *Imaginary You* that's an experiencer of any given moment, it grows the knowingness that the experiencing itself is what you are.

Doing any PMI at all will generally be a great aid to the seeker, but some ingredients seem to make PMI even more effective:

- A playful attitude
- A calm desire for the truth
- Curiosity
- Optimism
- Amusement
- Joy, wonder, and fascination

ALL OF THE above will make your PMI that much more powerful.

Any experiencing at all can be investigated. Seekers often begin by doing PMI with what are considered their negative experiencings, such as anger, stress, sadness, pain, etc., because the seeker most easily notices them. And that's a great place to begin.

PMI is a wonderful thing to do anytime, anywhere, but the power of the mundane moment should not be overlooked. When the *Imaginary You* isn't flexing its distaste about the present moment is an easy time to make your way into the purity of that moment.

When people ask about the *practice* of PMI, I more often describe it as the *play* of PMI; this occurs when a PMI confluence arises that allows it to happen. The power in the play is the soft-style, which is why it's not really a *method*—it's a *style*—a style of investigating the present moment.

The seeker is encouraged to play with soft-style questions whenever they desire,

such as:

- Can I find the one who thinks things shouldn't be the way they are?

- Can I find the one who is angry?

- Can I find the one who wants to awaken?

- Can I find the one who doesn't want to be separate?

- Can I find the one who doesn't want to suffer?

PMI OFFERS NO RESISTANCE. It's, "<u>*Yes*</u>, this is going on, <u>*And*</u> let's investigate it." The more you can approach these investigations like play, the lighter and more powerful your PMI becomes.

5

CONCLUSION

The Big Picture

"UPWARD, NOT NORTHWARD," WAS THE CLUE TO THE whole proof.

These were the instructions given to those living in a two-dimensional world called *Flatland*, whose seekers were trying to discover a three-dimensional world called *Spaceland*.

For those of us privileged enough to live in three dimensional space, "Upward, not northward," clarifies our direction quite well. But until a Flatlander has experienced, even briefly, a world of three dimensions, such pointings are mystifying.

A Flatlander could spend an entire lifetime never experiencing *upward*, unless the right circumstances occurred to help lift them off of their two-dimensional plane, and upward into space.

Edwin Abbot wrote the book, *Flatland*, in 1884, but the journey of the three-dimensional seekers in his short book is precisely similar to those of today's non-dual seekers.

"Attend to your configuration," is the maxim of the high priests who are against 3rd-dimensional seekers experiencing this thing called *space*. They don't want seekers to investigate the true nature of things.

Thus, the maxim for those seeking a conscious awakening must point them in a direction opposite of the Flatland high priests. For the non-dual seekers, the maxim is clear; "Investigate your present moment configuration, but do it soft-style, by asking the right questions."

Now You Know The Way

We began our spiritual journey by noting the difficulty in finding, "True places," which, "are not down in any map." Awakening is *undoubtedly* one of those places.

Present Moment Investigation will experientially show seekers of awakening that we're *always* already *it*. Because *it* is the actual experiencing of the present moment, there's *no way* not to be *it*. This glorious simplicity is stunning.

Awakening is a difference, not just in degree, but in *kind*, from those experiencing the world as a *seems to be* separate *Imaginary You*. Thus, the difficulty for the seeker is that most often they're using a nonexistent, imaginary self to try to discover that there's no imaginary self. Good imaginary luck!

A small number of spiritual concepts appear to be all that are required for the spiritual seeker to have a conscious awakening. Endless spiritual answers to seeker's questions tend to become an ever-growing Hydra of concepts that only reinforce the *Imaginary You*.

Hard-style, open-ended spiritual questions tend to sprout Hydra's of their own, each question growing ever more questions for the *Imaginary You* to nurture and grow into more and more concepts.

Too many concepts and too much information just reinforce the *Imaginary You* that the seeker needs to see through to awaken.

It's only the soft-style spiritual questions that funnel the seeker from conceptual spiritual seeking into the actual experiencing of that toward which all their spiritual concepts point.

This is because awakening is ultimately a negative process, and why it's only the right questions that will allow one to awaken.

The first negative is losing your identification with an

Imaginary You. The second negative is losing all your concepts about *what is* as you recognize the experiencing of the present moment as *what you are*.

Present Moment Investigation merely asks questions, which is why I call it *soft-style*. It asserts nothing, but it investigates everything. And the investigations lead to a place where there is freedom from the known; a place to *be* the experiencing of each moment *as* what you *are*.

Here's another example of soft-style PMI:

- Who seems to be having this experience?

- Can I find them if I look for them? (Then *actually* look for them in the body.)

- In the absence of a *seems to be* self, in the absence of an *Imaginary You*, does experiencing in your location continue?

- In the absence of an *Imaginary You*, is there any way you're *not* left *as* the experiencing of the present moment in your location?

- With the awareness of others having their own unique experiencings of the present moment in their locations, is there any way your experiencing is not part of a greater whole of experiencing going on?

- If we label the greater whole of experiencing *Oneness*, is there any way you're *not* the unique experiencing of Oneness in your location?

- As you're consciously aware of being Oneness playing within Oneness to experience Oneness in your location, what's it like to *be* the experiencing Oneness in each present moment?

BY JUST ASKING QUESTIONS, PMI leads the seeker to the experiencing of the present moment as what they are; what they've *always* been. They experience the *One Taste*; the taste of Oneness. They awaken.

When PMI becomes a habit, the One Taste will grow until you abide in the present moment experiencing as what you always already are. Once there's been the experiential recognition of the One Taste, and a soft-style way to revisit and grow the One Taste consistently, the playful habit will just become what gets done.

Despite the fact that there's no doer, no *Imaginary You*-er, PMI gets done. And the One Taste grows until you abide *as* what you *always already are*; the unique experiencing of Oneness in the present moment; *continually*.

Play with your PMI whenever the confluence arises. Relax and play. All is well. The One Taste is yours to revisit at any time.

"It's not down in any map; true places never are," but now you know the way to the One Taste, so visit often, until you abide there.

FREE EBOOK

If you enjoyed *Soft-Style Conscious Awakening*,
please consider leaving a review on Amazon
Even a line or two would be incredibly helpful:
Amazon US | Amazon UK

Gary Crowley's **FREE ebook,**
Why Most Non-Dual Seeking Fails,
is available to you right now at
www.GaryCrowley.com

ALSO BY GARY CROWLEY

From Here To Here, Turning Toward Enlightenment

Pass The Jelly, Tales Of Ordinary Enlightenment

Free eBook - Why Most Non-Dual Spiritual Seeking Fails

ABOUT THE AUTHOR

Gary Crowley has been a contemporary spiritual teacher since 2006 and a student of Eastern wisdom for over 30 years. His teachings are simple, direct, and most importantly, experiential. Gary views his job as providing the seeker with the missing "experiential assist" that will allow a conscious awakening. Gary's free eBook, *Why Most Non-Dual Spiritual Seeking Fails*, is available at www.GaryCrowley.com. Gary's previous two books, *From Here To Here, Turning Toward Enlightenment*, and *Pass The Jelly, Tales of Ordinary Enlightenment* have been highly praised for both their effectiveness as well as their memorable presentations.

Gary lives in Encinitas, California, just north of San Diego.

ACKNOWLEDGMENTS

First, a long overdue thank you to Jerry Katz of nonduality.com who has been nothing but supportive of my books from the first time I contacted him fifteen years ago, to my most recent contact regarding this book. Also, to Rick Archer whose BATGAP videos have allowed many a pilgrim on the path to happen upon my teachings over the years. And a very humble standing ovation of appreciation for Ike Allen, of Avaiya.com, whose unsolicited persistent positive promotion of my books has been a delightful occurrence since our first meeting thirteen years ago.

I'd also like to thank my friends and colleagues Mark Iglehart, Ande Anderson, Dan Millman, and Tom Thompson for their longtime support of all my books.

A special thanks to Fred Davis whose vast enthusiasm and support re-sparked the "author within," which made this book possible.

And editorial applause for Joan Schaublin whose grammatical dexterity and sense of humor while editing this playbook were greatly appreciated.

And lastly, thank you to Amber Flynn, whose big heart, dog loving ways, and professional level tech support allow everything in my life run more smoothly.

Made in the USA
Las Vegas, NV
14 January 2022

41403912R10070